Prelude to War

Massachusetts, South Carolina, and the
Decade of Disunion

Eleanor T. Whitfield

Copyright © Eleanor T. Whitfield, 2024.

All rights reserved.

Thankful to you for consenting to protected innovation guidelines by downloading this book through genuine methods and by not replicating, checking, or spreading any piece of this book.

Table of Contents

Introduction
Chapter 1: The Mexican War and New Territories
Chapter 2: The 1850 Compromise
Chapter 3: The Voices of a Generation: Calhoun, Webster, and Clay
Chapter 4 The Repeal of the Missouri Compromise
Chapter 5: Bleeding Kansas
Chapter 6: John Brown's Raid on Harpers Ferry
Chapter 7: The Secession Crisis
Chapter 8: Massachusetts: The Antislavery Epicenter
Chapter 9: South Carolina: The Cradle of Secession
Chapter 10: The Election of 1860 and Lincoln's Ascendancy
Chapter 11: The Final Days of the Union
Conclusion

Introduction

The Mexican War, which took place between 1846 and 1848, had a profound impact on the United States, resulting in a territorial expansion of nearly one-third.

The United States was awarded enormous additional areas as a result of the Treaty of Guadalupe Hidalgo, which brought an end to the battle. These new lands included portions of Colorado and additional Mexico, as well as the states of California, Nevada, Utah, and Arizona.

On the other hand, this expansion sparked heated arguments about the question of whether or not slavery should be extended into these new regions. As a result of the conflict, a difficult task was presented: how to incorporate these territories into the Union without further inflaming tensions amongst the various sections of the population.

Previously, the Missouri Compromise line of 1820 had sought to strike a balance between states that were free and those that were enslaved. The newly acquired territories were located south of this line.

An issue that became a flashpoint was the question of whether or not to permit slavery in these regions. This debate revealed the deep-seated divides that existed between the North and the South. Slavery was not allowed to expand across the northern states because of the rising abolitionist feeling in those areas.

Because their agricultural economies were based on slave labor, the southern states maintained that they had the right to extend this institution.

This argument over the destiny of the new territories laid the foundation for a succession of political and social crises that would eventually lead to the Civil War.

This widening gap in the country was exemplified by the states of Massachusetts and South Carolina. The state of Massachusetts became a center of abolitionist activity, with notable individuals like Frederick Douglass and William Lloyd Garrison at the forefront of the movement to abolish slavery.

The state became a symbol of the North's moral and political hostility to the institution. In sharp contrast, South Carolina's economy and culture were inextricably entwined with slavery. The state's elites, particularly John C. Calhoun, zealously defended their way of life and considered any challenge to slavery as an existential crisis. This difference between the firmly abolitionist Massachusetts and the adamantly pro-slavery South Carolina underlined the increasing regional tensions.

The 1850s demonstrated the fragility of American democracy. The Compromise of 1850, which contained policies like the Fugitive Slave Act, attempted to pacify both North and South but ultimately pleased neither.

The revocation of the Missouri Compromise by the Kansas-Nebraska Act of 1854 led to violent battles in "Bleeding Kansas," highlighting the instability of the slavery issue. The Supreme Court's Dred Scott decision in 1857 further exacerbated tensions by holding that African Americans could not be citizens and that Congress had no jurisdiction to outlaw slavery in the territories.

As the country faced these grave concerns, the political scene grew more fractured. The Democratic Party broke along sectional lines, and the newly established Republican Party, with its anti-slavery platform, gained influence in the North.

The debates and disputes of this decade emphasized a basic truth: democracy needs ongoing vigilance and compromise to thrive. The failure to resolve conflicts over slavery led to a breakdown in conversation and collaboration, leading the country towards disunion.

Chapter 1: The Mexican War and New Territories

The Mexican-American War, which raged from 1846 to 1848, was a major event in American history that changed the nation's borders and deepened the heated fight over slavery.

The conflict finished with the Treaty of Guadalupe Hidalgo, signed on February 2, 1848, which provided important territory gains to the United States.

This treaty transferred a large tract of territory from Mexico to the U.S., encompassing present-day California, Nevada, Utah, most of Arizona, and sections of New Mexico, Colorado, and Wyoming. This annexation, known as the Mexican Cession, contributed over 500,000 square miles to the United States, expanding its size by almost 25%.

The end of the war and the acquisition of these enormous areas were considered by many as a fulfillment of the nation's Manifest Destiny—the concept that Americans were destined to spread across the continent.

However, this fresh area also provoked quick and violent conflicts about the spread of slavery. The issue of whether these new areas would be free or slave-holding became a flashpoint, laying the scene for a decade of warfare that would eventually lead to the Civil War.

The Slavery Question in New Lands

The subject of slavery in the new territories was difficult and extremely polarizing. The Missouri Compromise of 1820 had previously set a boundary at 36°30' north latitude, with slavery outlawed in the territory north of this line and authorized south of it. However, the additional territories obtained from Mexico were both north and south of this line, creating doubts regarding the application of the Missouri Compromise to these new regions.

The Wilmot Proviso, offered in 1846 by Congressman David Wilmot of Pennsylvania, aimed to remedy this problem by suggesting that slavery be abolished in any area gained from Mexico.

Although the proviso passed the House of Representatives, it failed in the Senate, demonstrating the strong sectional division over slavery. The argument over the Wilmot Proviso showed the rising friction between the North, which primarily opposed the growth of slavery, and the South, which wished to defend and promote its particular institution.

As the additional territories were absorbed into the United States, many solutions developed to handle the slavery dilemma. One such notion was popular sovereignty, championed by Senator Lewis Cass of Michigan and subsequently by Senator Stephen A. Douglas of Illinois.

This ideology argued that the population of an area should determine the status of slaves themselves. While popular sovereignty was meant to give a democratic solution, it ultimately led to additional strife, notably in Kansas, where pro- and anti-slavery settlers battled brutally.

The Compromise of 1850 was another important effort to address the slavery problem in the new territories. Engineered by Senator Henry Clay and supported by other prominent senators like Daniel Webster and John C. Calhoun, the compromise included several key provisions: California was admitted as a free state, the territories of New Mexico and Utah were organized with the question of slavery to be decided by popular sovereignty, the slave trade (but not slavery itself) was abolished in Washington, D.C., and a more stringent Fugitive Slave Law was enacted.

While the Compromise of 1850 momentarily alleviated tensions, it also highlighted the increasing sectional split and prepared the way for additional wars.

Early Signs of Division

The Mexican-American War and its aftermath displayed early indicators of the approaching divide that would ultimately lead to the Civil War. The battle over the Wilmot Proviso and the Compromise of 1850 revealed the significant divides between the North and South over the future of slavery. These disparities were not just political but also significantly cultural and economic.

In the North, the burgeoning abolitionist movement fought for an end to slavery, perceiving it as morally abhorrent and economically backward.

The North's economy was increasingly focused on free labor and industrialization, which contrasted strongly with the South's dependence on slave labor and agriculture, notably the production of cotton. Abolitionist activists like William Lloyd Garrison, Frederick Douglass, and Harriet Beecher Stowe rallied public opinion against slavery, further splitting the country.

In contrast, the South considered slavery as crucial to its economic and social order. Southern elites contended that slavery was not only a constitutional right but also a positive benefit that produced stability and prosperity.

They felt that any limitation on the growth of slavery would imperil their way of life and lead to economic disaster. This anxiety was accentuated by the expanding political dominance of the North, which outperformed the South in population and economic capability.

The controversy over the spread of slavery into the new regions also had enormous political repercussions. The balance of power in the Senate, where each state had equal representation, was a key issue for both the North and the South. Each new state that joined the Union had the potential to upset this balance, either in favor of free or slave states. This made the issue of whether new areas would accept slavery a matter of national concern.

The early hints of conflict were further indicated by the formation of sectional political groups. The Free Soil Party, created in 1848, specifically opposed the introduction of slavery into the new areas, mirroring Northern concerns.

Meanwhile, Southern politicians gradually rallied around the protection of slavery, leading to the ultimate foundation of the Southern Democratic Party. These sectoral parties underlined the widening political and ideological gap that was fragmenting the country.

The Compromise of 1850, although momentarily soothing the waters, ultimately failed to solve the fundamental causes. The execution of the Fugitive Slave Law, which compelled the return of runaway slaves to their owners, angered Northern abolitionists and led to widespread opposition and bloodshed.

The publication of Harriet Beecher Stowe's "Uncle Tom's Cabin" in 1852 further inflamed Northern feelings against slavery, while Southern states strengthened their grasp on the institution, establishing legislation to reinforce their control over enslaved people.

As the country battled with the topic of slavery in the new territories, it became more evident that agreement was becoming more impossible to obtain. The early signals of separation that came from the Mexican-American War and its aftermath were harbingers of the bigger war to come. The discussions, legislation, and violent confrontations of the 1850s exposed the increasing gulf between North and South, laying the ground for the Civil War.

Chapter 2: The 1850 Compromise

The Compromise of 1850 was a bundle of five independent acts enacted by the United States Congress in September 1850, which defused a four-year political battle between slave and free states about the status of territories gained during the Mexican-American War. It was an elaborate and delicate endeavor to balance the interests of the Northern and Southern states and prevent a secession crisis.

Crafting the Compromise

The creation of the Compromise of 1850 was a momentous legislative endeavor headed by famous leaders such as Henry Clay, Daniel Webster, and Stephen A. Douglas. Henry Clay, renowned as the "Great Compromiser" for his involvement in the Missouri Compromise of 1820, submitted a series of resolutions to the Senate on January 29, 1850. These agreements intended to address the territorial and slavery problems emerging from the Mexican-American War.

The primary components of Clay's resolutions included:

Admission of California: California would be admitted to the Union as a free state, skipping the territorial stage and upsetting the balance between free and slave states in the Senate.

Territorial Status and Popular Sovereignty: The territories of New Mexico and Utah would be constituted without any formal ban on slavery, enabling the population of these territories to resolve the question of slavery via popular sovereignty.

Texas Boundary and Debt: Texas would abandon its claims to areas of New Mexico in exchange for federal absorption of its public debt.

Abolition of the Slave Trade in Washington D.C.: The slave trade, but not slavery itself, would be outlawed in the nation's capital.

A Stronger Fugitive Slave Law: A stricter Fugitive Slave Act would be implemented to address Southern worries over the loss of their property.

These initiatives sparked significant discussion in Congress, reflecting the wide differences within the nation. The discussion included emotional remarks, with Daniel Webster's famous "Seventh of March" address pushing for compromise and unity, while John C. Calhoun, representing the Southern interests, warned of the perils of disunion if Southern rights were not maintained.

Stephen A. Douglas, a young senator from Illinois, played a significant role in breaking the parliamentary logjam. Rather than seeking to approve Clay's resolutions as an omnibus package, Douglas campaigned for dividing the initiatives and approving them separately. This method was effective, and by September 1850, all five laws were implemented.

Strengthening the Fugitive Slave Law

One of the most contentious components of the Compromise of 1850 was the tightening of the Fugitive Slave Law. The original Fugitive Slave

Act of 1793 had proved unsuccessful, and Southern slaveholders were increasingly dissatisfied with the number of enslaved persons who fled to free states and the lack of assistance from Northern authorities.

The new Fugitive Slave Law of 1850 imposed tougher penalties on individuals who supported fugitive slaves and more severe conditions for their apprehension and return. Key features of the bill included:

Federal Commissioners: The law created a network of federal commissioners who were allowed to issue warrants for the apprehension of suspected runaway slaves and determine their status. These commissioners were given extra for decide in favor of slaveholders, leading to suspicions of prejudice.

No Jury Trials: Alleged runaway slaves were denied the right to a jury trial and could not testify on their behalf. This meant that the evidence of the claimant (the claimed slave owner) was frequently enough to restore a person to slavery.

Penalties for Assistance: Individuals who assisted fleeing slaves by providing food, shelter, or transportation risked harsh fines and imprisonment. This comprised both individual persons and authorities in free states.

Federal Enforcement: The legislation obligated all people to aid in the arrest and return of runaway slaves when called upon by federal officials. Local law enforcement in free states was required to participate, further angering Northern abolitionists.

The new legislation was considered a compromise to the South, assuring that their property rights in human chattel would be safeguarded even in free states. However, it also had the unforeseen consequence of mobilizing Northern resistance to slavery and bolstering the abolitionist cause.

Northern Outrage and Southern Satisfaction

The passage of the tougher Fugitive Slave Law sparked quick and furious responses. In the North, the measure was received with great fury and opposition. Abolitionists and free African Americans were especially enraged, perceiving the measure as a direct attack on their rights and liberties.

Abolitionist leaders including Frederick Douglass, Harriet Beecher Stowe, and William

Lloyd Garrison opposed the bill, holding public gatherings, printing pamphlets, and making speeches to raise opposition. Underground Railroad operators, including Harriet Tubman, redoubled their efforts to aid escaping slaves, facing harsh fines under the new rule.

In places like Boston, New York, and Philadelphia, enormous public demonstrations erupted. In several situations, Northern communities intentionally hindered the execution of the legislation. High-profile incidents, like as the apprehension of Anthony Burns in Boston, aroused hundreds of individuals who sought to rescue runaway slaves and prevent their return to the South

The fury also surfaced in the political sphere. Several Northern states established "personal liberty laws" aimed to offset the Fugitive Slave

Law. These state statutes offered legal safeguards for alleged fugitives and placed fines on state authorities who cooperated with federal enforcement attempts.

Conversely, in the South, the enhanced Fugitive Slave Law was mainly considered a tremendous triumph. Southern slaveholders felt gratified that their property rights were being maintained and that the federal government was making efforts to assure the return of fugitive slaves.

The law's approval was considered an essential counterweight to the admission of California as a free state, which had threatened to disturb the delicate balance of power in the Senate.

The joy in the South, however, was tempered by the understanding that the North was growing more opposed to slavery. The fierce opposition to the Fugitive Slave Law in free states underscored Southern suspicions that their way of life was in danger.

The Immediate Effects

The initial repercussions of the Compromise of 1850 were mixed. On one side, the measure succeeded in defusing the immediate situation and delayed the independence of Southern states.

The admittance of California as a free state and the establishment of the Utah and New Mexico territories under popular sovereignty briefly preserved the precarious equilibrium between free and slave states.

However, the Compromise also had some unexpected repercussions. The enactment of the tougher Fugitive Slave Law greatly alienated the North, boosting the expansion of the abolitionist movement and heightening sectional tensions. The vigorous execution of the law and the high-profile incidents of runaway slave recapture brought the cruelty of slavery into Northern awareness, prompting many who had previously been apathetic to become more aggressively opposed to the institution.

Moreover, the theory of popular sovereignty, meant to give a democratic solution to the problem of slavery in the territories, led to violent clashes, most notably in "Bleeding Kansas."

The effort to empower settlers to decide the status of slavery culminated in a proxy war between pro-slavery and anti-slavery groups, further splitting the country.

Politically, the Compromise of 1850 damaged the conventional party system. The Whig Party, profoundly split over the subject of slavery, started to crumble, while the Democratic Party also experienced internal struggle.

This time witnessed the birth of new political parties, such as the Free Soil Party and later the Republican Party, which would be built on an anti-slavery platform.

Chapter 3: The Voices of a Generation: Calhoun, Webster, and Clay

In the early to mid-19th century, three towering men dominated American politics, influencing the speech and direction of the country. John C. Calhoun, Daniel Webster, and Henry Clay, each with their views and methods, negotiated the dangerous political terrain of a country increasingly split over questions of states' rights, slavery, and national unity.

Their contributions and clashes left permanent traces on American history, embodying the era's intense debates and dramatic upheavals.

John C. Calhoun: The Southern Firebrand

John Caldwell Calhoun, born in 1782 in South Carolina, emerged as a strong voice for the Southern states and a fervent champion of states' rights and slavery. Calhoun's early career as a patriot and a War Hawk during the War of 1812 developed substantially as he became more affiliated with the Southern cause.

Calhoun's philosophy of nullification, which maintained that states had the power to invalidate federal legislation considered unconstitutional, was a direct challenge to federal authority.

This notion reached its apex during the Nullification Crisis of 1832-1833 when South Carolina tried to repeal the federal tariffs of 1828 and 1832. President Andrew Jackson's stern reaction, including the Force Bill allowing military action against South Carolina, pushed

Calhoun and his adherents to stand down. However, the crisis emphasized the increasing sectional gap and prepared the ground for future confrontations.

Calhoun's impassioned advocacy of slavery as a "positive good" further split the country. He maintained that slavery was advantageous for both slaves and slaveholders, offering a paternalistic rationale for the system.

His statements in the Senate presented a picture of Southern civilization that was profoundly in conflict with the increasing abolitionist movement in the North. Calhoun's conviction in the intrinsic inequality of races and his advocacy of the Southern way of life sealed his status as a firebrand who was immovable in his views.

Despite his contentious ideas, Calhoun was a great politician and orator, renowned even by his detractors for his brilliance and passion. He served as Vice President under both John Quincy Adams and Andrew Jackson, a rare achievement that displayed his political savvy.

Calhoun's death in 1850 did not reduce his impact; his theories continued to resonate with Southern leaders who subsequently seceded from the Union.

Daniel Webster: The Northern Orator

In sharp contrast to Calhoun stood Daniel Webster, born in 1782 in New Hampshire. Webster was one of the finest orators in American history, noted for his eloquence, brilliance, and unrelenting devotion to preserving the Union. His speeches, especially the famous "Second Reply to Hayne," were masterpieces of eloquence that emphasized the concepts of American nationalism and the primacy of the federal government.

Webster's career was defined by his legal skills and his term as a senator from Massachusetts. He played a crucial role in the important decisions before the Supreme Court, such as McCulloch v. Maryland and Gibbons v. Ogden, which helped determine the balance of power between state and federal governments.

Webster's arguments strengthened the concept that the Constitution constituted a binding compact among the states, thereby rejecting Calhoun's nullification thesis.

A staunch unionist, Webster played a vital part in the Compromise of 1850, a series of legislative measures aimed at quelling sectional hostilities. His support for the Fugitive Slave Act, however, harmed his image among many Northern abolitionists who considered it a betrayal of his anti-slavery views.

Webster's pragmatic attitude was influenced by his notion that maintaining the Union was important, even if it meant making concessions to the South.

Webster's influence as an orator and politician is timeless. His speeches continue to be studied for their rhetorical skill and their tremendous effect on American political philosophy. Webster died in 1852, leaving behind a legacy of loyalty to the Union and the ideas of constitutional governance.

Henry Clay: The Great Compromiser

Henry Clay, born in 1777 in Virginia, was a prominent player in American politics for over half a century. Known as the "Great Compromiser," Clay's political career was characterized by his attempts to bridge the sectional divide and establish common ground between the North and South.

His ability to make compromises won him a reputation as a statesman who emphasized the nation's stability before political objectives.

Clay's political path started in Kentucky, where he established himself as a distinguished lawyer and politician. He served as Speaker of the House, Senator, and Secretary of State under John Quincy Adams. Clay's American System, an economic plan that called for a strong national bank, protective tariffs, and internal reforms, sought to create national economic progress and unity.

Clay's most famous accomplishments were his involvement in the Missouri Compromise of 1820 and the Compromise of 1850. The Missouri Compromise intended to preserve the balance of power between free and slave states by admitting Missouri as a slave state and Maine as a free state, but barring slavery north of the 36°30' latitude. This delicate equilibrium was a temporary solution to the developing sectional rivalry.

The Compromise of 1850, which included provisions like the admission of California as a free state and the passage of a tougher Fugitive Slave Law, was Clay's last and most comprehensive attempt to fend off disunion. Despite his declining health, Clay's leadership was vital in navigating the difficult arguments and obtaining approval for the agreement.

Clay's impact as a mediator and a proponent of national unity is considerable. He was a pioneer of the Whig Party and a mentor to future political leaders such as Abraham Lincoln. Clay's death in 1852 signaled the end of an era, but his contributions to American politics and his attempts to avert civil war remained significant.

Their Legacies and Deaths

The deaths of Calhoun, Webster, and Clay in the early 1850s signified the departure of a generation of politicians who had defined the nation's early history. Their legacies are entwined with the events that led to the Civil

War, each reflecting distinct facets of the American experience.

Calhoun's steadfast advocacy of states' rights and slavery established the intellectual framework for Southern independence. His notions of nullification and state sovereignty would subsequently be used by the Confederacy in their rationale for breaking away from the Union.

Webster's fight for the Union and his superb oratory had a lasting effect on American political philosophy. His talks underlined the significance of a strong federal government and the perils of sectionalism. Webster's confidence in the Union as an inseparable institution influenced succeeding generations of leaders who struggled to maintain it during the Civil War.

Clay's attempts to build agreements revealed the possibilities of finding common ground even in the face of severe divides. His reputation as a statesman who prioritized unity and stability above politics is a monument to his loyalty to the American experiment. Clay's vision of a unified country, however, eventually proved inadequate to avoid the start of civil war.

Together, Calhoun, Webster, and Clay symbolized the complexity and paradoxes of antebellum America. Their lives and professions mirrored the intense disputes over slavery, states' rights, and national identity that would finally culminate in the Civil War. As towering leaders of their time, they left behind legacies that continue to define our knowledge of this vital moment in American history.

Chapter 4 The Repeal of the Missouri Compromise

The Missouri Compromise of 1820 was a historic deal in the early history of the United States, providing a temporary compromise to the sectional strife over the spread of slavery. Under this deal, Missouri was admitted as a slave state and Maine as a free state, preserving the balance between slave and free states in the Senate.

Furthermore, slavery was forbidden in all regions north of the 36°30' latitude line, except Missouri. This agreement was maintained for nearly three decades, but by the 1850s, it was evident that its stability was in danger.

The Kansas-Nebraska Act

The Kansas-Nebraska Act, presented by Senator Stephen A. Douglas in 1854, attempted to assist the establishment of the Kansas and Nebraska territories. Douglas, a great champion of popular sovereignty

—the belief that the population of a territory should resolve the question of slavery for themselves

—sought to extend this theory to the new territories.

The legislation advocated that the Missouri Compromise line be essentially overturned, enabling the matter of slavery to be settled by the people in each territory by popular vote.

Douglas's objectives were not solely ideological. The organization of these regions was vital for the building of a transcontinental railroad, which he felt would benefit his home state of Illinois and strengthen national unity. However, Douglas misjudged the strength of the sectional conflicts his plan would generate.

The Kansas-Nebraska Act provided that the status of slavery in the Kansas and Nebraska territories would be determined by the inhabitants, leading to a frontal confrontation over the future of slavery in the American West.

Popular Sovereignty and Its Discontents

The notion of popular sovereignty was meant to provide a democratic solution to the controversial subject of slavery. By enabling the settlers of a region to vote on whether to legalize slavery, it seemed to conform to the ideas of self-governance and majority rule. However, in actuality, it was fundamentally defective and led to enormous conflict and bloodshed.

The Kansas-Nebraska Act quickly split the country. In the North, it was considered a violation of the Missouri Compromise, which had been a sacred agreement for the containment of slavery.

Northern abolitionists and anti-slavery campaigners interpreted the measure as an effort to expand the institution of slavery into new regions where it had previously been outlawed. Their fury was apparent, with famous personalities such as Charles Sumner and William Lloyd Garrison denouncing the conduct in no uncertain terms.

In the South, the legislation was hailed by pro-slavery forces who viewed it as a chance to extend the institution of slavery and safeguard their economic interests. Southern politicians and landowners were eager to push slavery into the lush areas of the West, considering it crucial for the ongoing expansion and prosperity of their agricultural economy.

The immediate aftermath of the Kansas-Nebraska Act was a rush of both pro-slavery and anti-slavery settlers into Kansas, each side seeking to influence the outcome of the approaching vote. This inflow laid the atmosphere for a period of intense and frequently deadly strife known as "Bleeding Kansas."

The Prelude to Conflict

"Bleeding Kansas" became the physical symbol of the national battle over slavery. Pro-slavery settlers, many of whom came from nearby Missouri, battled with anti-slavery settlers, who were mostly from the North. The land immediately became a battlefield, with both sides striving to impose their supremacy via a mix of political intrigue and plain bloodshed.

The first significant flashpoint occurred with the elections for the territory assembly in 1855. Pro-slavery troops, called "Border Ruffians," came into Kansas from Missouri to vote illegally, securing a pro-slavery majority in the legislature.

This led to the foundation of a pro-slavery administration in Lecompton, which adopted laws favorable to slavery. In response, anti-slavery settlers built up their parallel government in Topeka, resulting in a scenario where two competing governments claimed sovereignty over the province.

The violence intensified further with the notorious "Sack of Lawrence" in May 1856, when pro-slavery soldiers assaulted and robbed the free-state bastion of Lawrence, Kansas. This act of violence was greeted with revenge by radical abolitionist John Brown, who led a raid on the pro-slavery colony at Pottawatomie Creek, brutally murdering five people. Brown's actions increased the conflict and split the region even more.

The national effect of the struggle in Kansas was enormous. It showed the fundamental weaknesses in the notion of popular sovereignty and indicated that the subject of slavery could not be handled via democratic methods alone. The bloodshed and anarchy in Kansas functioned as a microcosm of the greater sectional war and anticipated the approaching Civil War.

Political and Social Ramifications

The Kansas-Nebraska Act had important political and social repercussions beyond the immediate conflict in Kansas. It resulted in the demise of the Whig Party, which had been one of the two main political parties in the United States.

The party's failure to adopt a consistent position on the subject of slavery and its growth led to its breakup. In its stead, the Republican Party developed and established a platform of resisting the extension of slavery into the western provinces.

The Republican Party swiftly gained popularity in the North, gaining former Whigs, Free Soilers, and anti-slavery Democrats. The party's quick ascent to prominence mirrored the widening sectional split and the rising polarization of American politics.

The Kansas-Nebraska Act and the bloodshed it unleashed had a key effect in establishing the political landscape of the United States in the years leading up to the Civil War.

In the South, the legislation reinforced pro-slavery sentiment and cemented the determination to maintain and extend the institution of slavery. Southern politicians and landowners hailed the measure as a win and were encouraged in their efforts to reject any moves to reduce or abolish slavery.

The cultural influence of the Kansas-Nebraska Act was likewise substantial. It widened the ideological rift between the North and South, making reconciliation more impossible.

The moral and ethical conflicts surrounding slavery grew increasingly entrenched, with both sides growing more radical in their beliefs. The notion of a single country was increasingly eclipsed by the reality of two diverse and incompatible communities.

Chapter 5: Bleeding Kansas

The mid-1850s constituted one of the most violent and chaotic eras in American history. Known as "Bleeding Kansas," this period saw the territory of Kansas become a battlefield between pro-slavery and anti-slavery forces, both battling for power over whether the state would join the Union as a free or slave state.

This war was not only a regional conflict but a microcosm of the wider national argument over slavery, eventually influencing the path of American history.

The Struggle for Kansas

The Kansas-Nebraska Act of 1854, proposed by Senator Stephen A. Douglas, sought to assist the building of a transcontinental railroad and encourage western development. It recommended that the territories of Kansas and Nebraska be constituted under the basis of popular sovereignty, letting the residents of each area determine whether to legalize slavery.

This measure essentially reversed the Missouri Compromise of 1820, which had restricted slavery north of the 36°30' parallel, and revived sectional hostilities between the North and the South.

The war for Kansas started almost immediately after the act's adoption, as both pro-slavery and anti-slavery people flocked into the territory to influence the result of the first elections. Pro-slavery migrants, largely from Missouri, traveled to Kansas to vote illegally, intending to build a government friendly to their cause. This led to the construction of a pro-slavery territory legislature, which adopted severe pro-slavery policies, including fines for helping fleeing slaves and promoting abolition.

In reaction, anti-slavery pioneers, known as Free-Staters, founded their government in Topeka, establishing a competing constitution that abolished slavery. This dual administration system heightened tensions and created an atmosphere for deadly conflicts. Both sides engaged in a propaganda war, sending pamphlets and newspaper pieces to the East to raise support and cash for their respective objectives.

Violence and Vengeance

The violence in Kansas evolved into a full-scale guerilla war, with both pro-slavery and anti-slavery troops committing atrocities. One of the oldest and most noteworthy instances was the Sack of Lawrence on May 21, 1856. Lawrence, an anti-slavery bastion, was besieged by a pro-slavery mob, who stole and torched businesses, damaged printing presses, and frightened inhabitants.

This episode was a turning moment, revealing the extent to which pro-slavery forces were ready to go to demonstrate their supremacy.

In retribution, the abolitionist John Brown led a small number of men in the Pottawatomie Massacre on May 24-25, 1856. Brown, an ardent believer in the abolitionist cause, planned to revenge the Sack of Lawrence and strike terror into pro-slavery people. His crew ruthlessly slaughtered five pro-slavery settlers at Pottawatomic Creek, cutting them to death with broadswords. This act of revenge further exacerbated the battle, resulting in additional killing and reprisals from both sides.

The conflict persisted into 1856, with several skirmishes and assaults on communities. One notable conflict was the conflict of Black Jack on June 2, 1856, when John Brown's troops met with pro-slavery militia, culminating in a Free-State victory.

Another notable encounter was the Battle of Osawatomie on August 30, 1856, when Brown's soldiers were beaten but managed to inflict substantial fatalities on their opponents, increasing the morale of the anti-slavery movement.

These acts were not isolated episodes but part of a greater pattern of violence and retaliation that plagued Kansas. The land became a symbol of the widening separation between North and South, with both sides considering the fight as a test of their respective beliefs. The bloodshed in Kansas also had a profound psychological influence on the country, indicating the potential for sectional animosity to escalate into open combat.

The Impact on National Politics

The turbulence in Kansas had enormous ramifications for national politics, affecting the establishment of political parties and altering the debate on slavery.

The Kansas-Nebraska Act and the accompanying bloodshed led to the demise of the Whig Party, which had been unable to unite its Northern and Southern divisions. This political realignment cleared the way for the creation of the Republican Party, formed in 1854 on an anti-slavery platform.

The Republican Party, formed of former Whigs, Free-Soilers, and anti-slavery Democrats, seized on the fury over Bleeding Kansas to acquire electoral momentum. The party's position opposing the spread of slavery resonated with Northern supporters, who considered the events in Kansas as proof of the Slave Power's aggressiveness.

The Republicans' performance in the 1856 elections, when their nominee John C. Frémont gained a major share of the Northern vote, illustrated the widening sectional division.

Bleeding Kansas also had a direct influence on the career of Stephen A. Douglas. As the author of the Kansas-Nebraska Act, Douglas suffered severe reactions from Northern Democrats, who felt misled by his support for popular sovereignty. The violence in Kansas damaged Douglas's premise that popular sovereignty could settle the slavery question peacefully, harming his image and reducing his influence within the Democratic Party.

The events in Kansas also affected the 1856 presidential election, which saw James Buchanan, a Democrat, barely beat John C. Frémont. Buchanan's win did nothing to ease the situa

Chapter 6: John Brown's Raid on Harpers Ferry

John Brown's attack on Harpers Ferry looms as one of the most crucial and divisive events leading up to the American Civil War. This brazen effort to encourage a slave insurrection deepened the nation's already combustible tensions, driving it closer to disunion and bloodshed.

Below, we go into the nuances of Brown's plot and execution, the immediate implications, the Southern concerns and Northern responses, and the continuing significance of the raid.

John Brown's Plan and Execution

John Brown, a zealous abolitionist, thought that violent action was essential to remove slavery

60

from the United States. By 1859, he had conceived a daring strategy to strike at the core of the institution. Brown wanted to take the government arsenal at Harpers Ferry, Virginia (now West Virginia), acquire its huge store of firearms, and distribute them to enslaved people in the area. He envisioned that this would spark a broad slave insurrection, eventually leading to the abolition of slavery.

Brown painstakingly organized the attack, amassing a small group of 21 men, including five African Americans, who shared his fervor for the cause. They convened in a leased farmhouse in Maryland, a few miles from Harpers Ferry, where they planned for the attack. Brown's scheme was ambitious but flawed: he overestimated the eagerness of enslaved people to join the revolt and underestimated the rapidity of the federal and local reaction.

On the night of October 16, 1859, Brown and his men crossed the Potomac River and entered Harpers Ferry. They swiftly captured the armory, along with numerous hostages, including Colonel Lewis Washington, a great-grandnephew of George Washington. Brown felt that taking notable hostages would delay any quick retribution and provide time for the insurrection to develop.

However, the early triumph was short-lived. Brown's soldiers were quickly hemmed down by local militia and furious citizens. By the next morning, news of the attack had reached Washington, D.C., and federal forces, headed by Colonel Robert E. Lee, were ordered to quash the revolt. After a two-day confrontation, during which many of Brown's men were killed or injured, the surviving invaders were overcome. Brown himself was arrested, injured, and put into jail.

Immediate Repercussions

The immediate aftermath of the raid was chaotic and brutal. Ten of Brown's men were slain, including two of his sons. Brown and six others were apprehended and swiftly placed on trial for treason, murder, and instigating a slave uprising.

Brown's trial, conducted in neighboring Charles Town, Virginia, gained national notice. Despite his wounds, Brown presented himself with dignity and strong conviction, utilizing the courtroom as a platform to decry slavery and call for its abolition.

The trial finished rapidly, with Brown being convicted guilty on all charges. On December 2, 1859, he was executed by hanging. His calm manner and eloquent dying remarks made him become a martyr for the abolitionist cause.

Brown's execution aroused anti-slavery sentiment in the North, where he was regarded as a hero and martyr, while the South saw him as a homicidal fanatic bent on starting a race war.

Southern Fears and Northern Reactions

The attack on Harpers Ferry sent shockwaves across the South, heightening previous worries of a major slave uprising. Southern slaveholders had long had fears about the likelihood of uprisings, and Brown's actions verified their darkest nightmares. The South reacted with heightened security measures, additional patrols, and greater restrictions over enslaved people. The raid also reinforced demands for secession, as many Southerners feared that continuing in the Union would only lead to further Northern-instigated bloodshed and turmoil.

In the North, responses were more complicated. While many abolitionists hailed Brown's willingness to risk his life for the cause, others were more cautious and apprehensive about the use of violence and its possible implications.

Prominent personalities such as Frederick Douglass and Henry David Thoreau commended Brown, with Thoreau notably making a speech titled "A Plea for Captain John Brown," in which he complimented Brown's moral heroism and criticized the government for defending slavery.

The political repercussions were tremendous. Northern backing for Brown further alienated the South and worsened sectional tensions. The raid and its aftermath became a flashpoint in the 1860 presidential election, with Southern Democrats exploiting it to imply that the North was bent on destroying their way of life.

Abraham Lincoln, the Republican nominee, distanced himself from Brown's actions but denounced slavery as a moral crime, a position that soothed abolitionists while frightening Southern supporters.

The Raid's Legacy

John Brown's attack on Harpers Ferry made an enduring imprint on American history. Though it failed to fulfill its immediate objective of sparking a slave uprising, it succeeded in bringing the nation's deep-seated disputes over slavery to the forefront of public awareness. Brown's acts and subsequent execution reinforced the moral and political divides between the North and South, leading to the secession crisis and the onset of the Civil War.

Brown's legacy is varied. In the North, he is generally regarded as a martyr and a symbol of the abolitionist movement. His desire to take direct action against an unfair system has inspired numerous activists and reformers.

In the South, however, he is typically presented as a terrorist whose acts threatened lives and property, bolstering the view that slavery was required to preserve social order. Historians continue to question Brown's effect and the ethics of his approach. Some consider him as a predecessor to subsequent civil rights activists who utilized direct action to combat institutional injustice, while others see him as a cautionary figure whose turn to violence illustrates the risks of fanaticism.

Regardless of one's opinion, Brown's assault on Harpers Ferry certainly played a major part in the events leading up to the Civil War, acting as a trigger for the eventual breach between North and South.

Chapter 7:The Secession Crisis

In the aftermath of Abraham Lincoln's election in November 1860, South Carolina found itself at a vital juncture. The state has long been a hotbed of separatist ism, motivated by a heavy dependence on slavery and a firm adherence to states' rights.

The election of a president who was viewed as opposed to the institution of slavery was the last straw for many South Carolinians.

On December 20, 1860, South Carolina became the first state to separate from the Union. This decision was not taken lightly; it was the product of years of rising tensions between the North and the South. South Carolina's authorities, especially Governor Francis W. Pickens and key people like Robert Barnwell Rhett and James Chesnut Jr., had been preparing for this moment. The state's Declaration of the Immediate Causes, which Induce and Justify the Secession of South Carolina from the Federal Union, highlighted their concerns, alleging abuses of states' rights and the perceived danger to slavery.

The secession conference, held in Charleston, was a momentous event, distinguished by speeches and resolutions that underlined the urgency of breaking away from the Union.

The tone was a blend of seriousness and ardent nationalism. For many South Carolinians, secession was perceived as a defense of their way of life and a preemptive strike against Northern encroachment.

The Secession of Other Southern States

South Carolina's independence sparked a chain reaction among the Southern states. Mississippi was the next to secede, on January 9, 1861, followed by Florida, Alabama, Georgia, Louisiana, and Texas.

Each state had its secession convention, when delegates discussed and finally chose to leave the Union. These conventions typically reflected the ideas stated by South Carolina, especially the protection of slavery and states' rights.

In Mississippi, for instance, the Declaration of Secession specifically declared that the state's position was "thoroughly identified with the institution of slavery." Georgia's proclamation criticized the North's actions and policies as antagonistic to the South's way of life. Each state's choice was inspired by a mix of economic concerns, political philosophy, and a feeling of shared identity with other slaveholding states.

These early secessions were mainly peaceful, with state militias assuming possession of federal facilities inside their boundaries. However, the mood was fraught with expectations and worry about the future. The seceding states started to contact and cooperate, establishing the basis for a new governmental entity.

The Formation of the Confederacy

On February 4, 1861, delegates from the seceded states convened in Montgomery, Alabama, to organize a new government. This conference led to the foundation of the Confederate States of America (CSA). The delegates developed a constitution, primarily modeled on the U.S. Constitution but with important modifications that stressed states' autonomy and maintained the institution of slavery.

Jefferson Davis, a former U.S. senator and secretary of war from Mississippi, was chosen as the temporary president of the Confederacy, with Alexander H. Stephens of Georgia as vice president. Davis was inaugurated on February 18, 1861. His leadership was viewed as important to the fledgling Confederacy, given his military expertise and political skill.

The Confederate Constitution was enacted on March 11, 1861. It nearly followed its U.S. equivalent but added critical articles that protected slavery and curtailed the central government's authority, reflecting the states' rights doctrine that had spurred independence.

The new administration rapidly went about organizing its military and diplomatic activities, seeking recognition and help from other countries, primarily Great Britain and France.

Montgomery served as the Confederacy's initial capital, but it was quickly transferred to Richmond, Virginia, following that state's independence in April 1861. Richmond's strategic and symbolic significance made it an obvious option, and its closeness to Washington, D.C., highlighted the approaching confrontation between the Union and the Confederacy.

The Union's Response

The Union, commanded by President Abraham Lincoln, faced an unprecedented crisis. Lincoln, inaugurated on March 4, 1861, was determined to maintain the Union. His inauguration speech aimed to soothe the South by ensuring that he had no desire to meddle with slavery where it existed. However, he also firmly asserted that secession was unlawful and that he would enforce federal laws in all states.

The first big test of Lincoln's determination came with the situation at Fort Sumter, a federal fort in Charleston Harbor. Despite South Carolina's secession, the fort remained under Union hands, signifying federal power in the South.

As supplies at the fort decreased, Lincoln faced a tough dilemma. Resupplying the fort may trigger a military reaction from the Confederacy while leaving it would signal weakness.

Lincoln chose to deploy a relief mission to Fort Sumter. This decision was considered an act of aggression by the Confederacy, and on April 12, 1861, Confederate soldiers under General P.G.T. Beauregard fired on the fort, signaling the commencement of the Civil War. After a 34-hour bombardment, Major Robert Anderson, the Union commander, abandoned the fort.

The assault on Fort Sumter energized the North. Lincoln asked for 75,000 volunteers to quash the insurrection, resulting in a surge of patriotism and enrollment throughout the Union states. However, this move also compelled the other slaveholding nations to select sides.

Virginia, Arkansas, Tennessee, and North Carolina seceded and joined the Confederacy, while border states like Missouri, Kentucky, and Maryland experienced internal divides and remained nominally in the Union, but with strong Confederate sympathies.

Lincoln's government rapidly proceeded to safeguard Washington, D.C., and the border states, knowing their strategic significance. The martial rule was proclaimed in Maryland, and Union soldiers guaranteed the state would not secede, therefore keeping the capital from being encircled by Confederate territory.

The Union also started pursuing a plan known as the Anaconda Plan, created by General Winfield Scott, which sought to blockade Southern ports and acquire control of the Mississippi River, thus squeezing the economic life out of the Confederacy.

This plan, along with a series of military conflicts, signaled the beginning of a protracted and violent struggle that would test the endurance and ideals of both the Union and the Confederacy.

Chapter 8:Massachusetts: The Antislavery Epicenter

Massachusetts, long a paragon of progressive thinking and activity, became the furnace of the antislavery movement in the United States. The state's metamorphosis as the nation's antislavery powerhouse was propelled by a mix of moral zeal, religious beliefs, and a vibrant network of abolitionist leaders and organizations.

Early Abolitionist Sentiments

The origins of abolitionism in Massachusetts may be traced back to the early 19th century when religious revivalism inspired a surge of moral and social reform groups. The Second Great Awakening, with its stress on individual piety and social purity, provided the basis for a developing abolitionist spirit. Massachusetts pastors and laypeople alike started to consider slavery as a grave moral evil that needed to be abolished.

Key Figures and Their Contributions

William Lloyd Garrison emerged as one of the most prominent and radical voices in the Massachusetts abolitionist movement. In 1831, Garrison created ***The Liberator***, an uncompromising antislavery journal that fought for rapid freedom and equal rights for African Americans.

Garrison's unrelenting lobbying and passionate eloquence energized the abolitionist movement and attracted public attention to the evils of slavery.

Garrison was quickly joined by other significant personalities, notably Frederick Douglass, a former slave whose remarkable oratory and writings offered direct evidence of the cruel reality of slavery.

Douglass's autobiography, ***Narrative of the Life of Frederick Douglass, an American Slave***, published in 1845, is a landmark piece in the abolitionist canon. His eloquence and moral power made him a strong spokesman for the abolitionist cause.

Another major contributor was Harriet Beecher Stowe, whose book ***Uncle Tom's Cabin*** (1852) dramatically altered popular opinion. The book's graphic description of the misery of enslaved people sparked deep emotions and rallied many Northerners against slavery. Though Stowe was not a Massachusetts resident, her work was warmly welcomed and supported by the state's abolitionist community.

Women also played a major part in the Massachusetts abolitionist struggle. Figures like Lydia Maria Child, Maria Weston Chapman, and the Grimké sisters (Angelina and Sarah) were crucial in forming antislavery groups, producing significant publications, and pushing for both abolition and women's rights. Their actions served to extend the basis of the movement and guarantee that the battle against slavery was inclusive and multidimensional.

Abolitionist Organizations

Massachusetts was home to numerous significant abolitionist groups that coordinated efforts and amplified the voices of individual campaigners. The Massachusetts Anti-Slavery

Society, formed in 1835, became a significant focus for abolitionist action. It staged lectures, rallies, and petition drives, bringing together a varied coalition of people devoted to eradicating slavery.

The American Anti-Slavery Society, while a national organization, had a significant presence in Massachusetts and worked closely with local organizations. These groups frequently faced violent resistance and legal challenges, but they persevered, utilizing the press, public gatherings, and political lobbying to keep the problem of slavery at the forefront of national awareness.

Political Maneuvering and Disputes

The abolitionist movement in Massachusetts was not restricted to grassroots action; it also had substantial ramifications for political maneuvering and disputes at both the state and national levels.

The Liberty Party and Free Soil Movement

As the abolitionist movement gathered speed, it started to have an enormous impact on the political scene. The Liberty Party, created in 1840, was one of the earliest political parties committed to the abolitionist movement. While it did not achieve great electoral success, it provided the framework for later important antislavery political campaigns.

By the late 1840s, the Free Soil Party developed, campaigning for the ban of slavery in the newly gained territory from the Mexican War. The party's motto, "Free Soil, Free Speech, Free Labor, and Free Men," resonated with many Massachusetts voters who were worried about the growth of slavery and its influence on free labor. Prominent Massachusetts politicians, including Charles Sumner and John P. Hale, became key advocates in the Free Soil Party, utilizing their positions to press for antislavery laws and stronger political representation for abolitionists.

The Republican Party and Radical Abolitionists

The 1850s witnessed the emergence of the Republican Party, which swiftly became the political home for many former Whigs, Free Soilers, and abolitionists.

Massachusetts was a bastion for the new party, which had a platform that opposed the introduction of slavery into the territories. Figures like Sumner and Henry Wilson, both

Massachusetts senators, played significant roles in establishing the party's ideas and rhetoric.

Sumner, in particular, became recognized for his ardent and sometimes heated lectures against slavery. In 1856, he made his famous "Crime Against Kansas" speech, criticizing the Kansas-Nebraska Act and its writers, particularly South Carolina Senator Andrew Butler.

Sumner's remark was so incendiary that it sparked a violent reaction from Representative Preston Brooks of South Carolina, who viciously caned Sumner on the Senate floor. This action, known as the Caning of Sumner, further split the country and underlined the fundamental conflicts over slavery.

State-Level Initiatives and Legislation

At the state level, Massachusetts took many actions to oppose the expansion of slavery and assist abolitionist activities. The state created personal liberty laws aimed at safeguarding runaway slaves and freeing African Americans from being abducted and sold into slavery.

These statutes directly challenged the federal Fugitive Slave Act, resulting in legal and political battles between state and federal authorities.

Massachusetts also became a significant battlefield in the dispute against the spread of slavery into another territory. The state's legislators and activists were in the vanguard of attempts to block the admission of additional slave states and to advocate the entrance of free states, therefore shifting the balance of power in Congress.

The State's engagement in National Politics

Massachusetts' engagement in national politics during the decade of disunion was defined by its persistent resistance to slavery and its attempts to sway the national discussion.

Notable Senators and Members

Massachusetts sent numerous notable senators and members to Congress who played crucial roles in the antislavery struggle. Beyond Charles Sumner, Henry Wilson acted as a significant champion for abolition and subsequently became Vice President under Ulysses S. Grant.

Their speeches, legislative measures, and political methods were crucial in putting the topic of slavery at the forefront of national politics.

The Influence of Public Opinion

The strong abolitionist feeling in Massachusetts had a profound influence on national public opinion. The state's publications, pamphlets, and public speeches were extensively circulated, influencing antislavery sentiment throughout the North.

Massachusetts' intellectual and cultural output, from Emerson's essays to Thoreau's civil disobedience, provided philosophical underpinnings for the abolitionist cause and inspired activists nationwide.

Collaboration with Other States

Massachusetts also collaborated with other Northern states to form a united front against the spread of slavery. The state's leaders worked closely with their counterparts in states like New

York, Pennsylvania, and Ohio, exchanging ideas and supporting each other's attempts to resist pro-slavery laws and legislation.

Massachusetts' position as the antislavery hub was multidimensional, combining grassroots movement, legislative maneuvering, and important national leadership. The state's abolitionist groups and leaders were vital in rallying public opinion and fighting for legislative reform.

The political disputes and maneuvering inside Massachusetts not only molded the state's posture but also had important repercussions for national politics, adding considerably to the tensions that eventually led to the Civil War. Through its unshakable devotion to the abolitionist cause, Massachusetts played a vital role in the nation's effort to abolish slavery and preserve the Union.

Chapter 9: South Carolina: The Cradle of Secession

South Carolina's economy in the mid-19th century was heavily ingrained in the system of slavery. The state's agricultural environment was dominated by huge estates that farmed cash crops including rice, indigo, and, most importantly, cotton.

The advent of the cotton gin in 1793 drastically boosted the need for slave labor since it allowed for the more efficient processing of cotton. By the 1850s, cotton had become the core of South Carolina's economy, and the state was one of the largest cotton producers in the United States.

The prosperity of cotton and other cash crops produced an economic structure that was primarily dependent on the labor of enslaved African Americans. Plantations were enormous, self-sustaining businesses where slaves not only worked the fields but also performed a range of skilled and unskilled labor.

The riches created by this system centralized authority in the hands of a tiny elite class of white landowners, who held the bulk of the slaves and the most productive land.

This economic necessity of slavery made the white elite passionately protective of the institution. They considered any challenge to slavery as a direct threat to their economic wealth and social position. The abolitionist movements and rising antislavery attitudes in the North were viewed as existential dangers. South Carolinians thought that their way of life, established 1793 based on slavery, was under threat.

Political Leaders and Secessionists

South Carolina's political scene was controlled by fervent proponents of slavery and states' rights. Among the most noteworthy characters was John C. Calhoun, a strong proponent of nullification and a fervent champion of the Southern way of life.

Calhoun's philosophy of nullification, which maintained that states had the power to nullify federal legislation considered unconstitutional, laid the ground for the separatist rhetoric that would eventually dominate South Carolina politics.

Calhoun's impact continued beyond his lifetime, as his principles were championed by future generations of South Carolina leaders. Men like Robert Barnwell Rhett, dubbed as the "Father of Secession," and James Henry Hammond carried further Calhoun's legacy.

Rhett was especially vociferous about the necessity for Southern states to express their independence from the Union, and he played a vital role in the secession effort.

Hammond, another significant figure, was famed for his "King Cotton" speech, which embodied the South's conviction in the economic strength of cotton and its relevance to the world economy. This statement emphasized the South's conviction that its economic clout would defend its interests, including the maintenance of slavery.

The political atmosphere in South Carolina was typified by a growing feeling of urgency and militancy. Pro-secession politicians gained popularity, and the language of states' rights and Southern independence grew more militant. These leaders felt that the best way to defend their economic interests and way of life was by secession from the Union.

The Move Toward Disunion

The march toward disunion in South Carolina was not a sudden change but a culmination of decades of political and economic conflicts. The Compromise of 1850, which contained the Fugitive Slave Act, momentarily quelled certain tensions but also heightened enmity. The statute demanded that fugitive slaves be returned to their owners even if they were discovered in free states, which infuriated abolitionists and reinforced Northern hostility to the system of slavery.

The Kansas-Nebraska Act of 1854, which essentially invalidated the Missouri Compromise by empowering territories to determine the question of slavery via popular sovereignty, further exacerbated tensions.

The violent encounters in "Bleeding Kansas" revealed the wide national division and the possibility for violence. South Carolinians considered these events as proof of Northern hostility and a direct danger to their way of life.

The Dred Scott decision in 1857, which determined that African Americans could not be citizens and that Congress had no jurisdiction to ban slavery in the territories, momentarily invigorated the South. However, it also mobilized Northern resistance and further split the country.

John Brown's attack on Harpers Ferry in 1859 marked a turning point. Brown's effort to stir a slave uprising sent shockwaves across the South, fueling concerns of a mass insurrection. In South Carolina, the invasion was regarded as a direct assault on their civilization and strengthened support for independence.

The election of Abraham Lincoln in 1860 was the ultimate spark for South Carolina's secession. Lincoln's anti-slavery program, while not immediately harmful to slavery where it already existed, was considered a precursor of the abolitionist movement. South Carolinians thought that during Lincoln's administration, their rights and way of life would be methodically undermined.

In December 1860, after Lincoln's election, South Carolina became the first state to separate from the Union. The decision was taken at a conference convened in Charleston when delegates voted overwhelmingly for independence.

The secession proclamation highlighted the alleged injustices and dangers presented by the Northern states and the federal government, portraying independence as a vital act of self-preservation.

The tendency toward disunion was fuelled by a mix of economic incentives, political ideology, and social anxieties. South Carolina's leaders were resolute in their opinion that secession was the only feasible alternative to safeguard their economy and way of life from the alleged encroachments of the North. Their acts created a precedent, and within months, other Southern states followed likewise, leading to the creation of the Confederacy and the commencement of the Civil War.

Chapter 10: The Election of 1860 and Lincoln's Ascendancy

The political environment of the United States in the lead-up to the 1860 presidential election was defined by widening differences and rising tensions. The 1850s witnessed a succession of events that escalated the sectional struggle between the North and the South, especially centered around the question of slavery.

The Mexican War and subsequent territory gains revived the argument over whether new republics would be free or slave states. The Compromise of 1850, the Kansas-Nebraska Act, and the Dred Scott decision each further split the country.

The political parties themselves were disintegrating under the pressure. The Whig Party had collapsed, partly owing to internal disputes over slavery. The Democratic Party, once a uniting force, was now divided among Northern and Southern divisions.

The newly created Republican Party, founded in the mid-1850s, had swiftly acquired favor in the North with its stance opposing the spread of slavery into the territories.

By 1860, the United States was teetering on the edge of disunion. The political environment was one of suspicion, dread, and rising animosity. Southern states thought their way of life, which was mainly based on slavery, was in immediate danger. Meanwhile, Northern states, propelled by a rising abolitionist feeling, were desperate to halt the expansion of slavery. This acrimonious climate laid the setting for one of the most consequential elections in American history.

Lincoln's Campaign and Election

Abraham Lincoln, a relatively insignificant Illinois lawyer and former legislator, emerged as a key figure in the Republican Party. His passionate arguments against the spread of slavery and his confrontations with Stephen Douglas during the 1858 Illinois Senate campaign had won him national notoriety. Despite losing the Senate contest, Lincoln's performances reinforced his image as a charismatic speaker and conscientious leader.

The Republican Party, assembling in Chicago in May 1860, picked Lincoln as their presidential candidate on the third vote, preferring him over other renowned contenders including William

Seward and Salmon Chase. Lincoln's moderate attitude on slavery, along with his Western upbringing, made him an attractive candidate who might take important swing states.

Lincoln's message was straightforward and resonated with many Northerners: resistance to the expansion of slavery into the territories, support for a transcontinental railroad, and the promotion of free labor. His campaign slogan, "Free soil, free labor, free men," summarized the Republican vision for America's future. The party's objective was to solidify support in the North and avoid alienating prospective supporters with strong abolitionist rhetoric.

The Democratic Party, bitterly split, staged two separate conventions. Northern Democrats nominated Stephen Douglas, who pushed for popular sovereignty—the premise that the citizens of each area should determine the question of slavery for themselves. Southern Democrats, however, rejected Douglas's stance and chose John C. Breckinridge, who favored federal protection of slavery in the territories. This schism seriously harmed the Democratic Party's prospects in the election.

Additionally, a fourth group, the Constitutional Union group, developed, composed mostly of former Whigs and Know-Nothings. They selected John Bell and concentrated on maintaining the Union and honoring the Constitution without taking a firm position on slavery.

The campaign was robust and intensive, with Lincoln's team adopting novel techniques such as the widespread use of railroads for travel and the distribution of millions of campaign posters, pamphlets, and newspapers. Lincoln personally stayed in Springfield, Illinois, maintaining a dignified and quiet demeanor while his supporters energetically campaigned on his behalf.

The election outcomes were crucial. Lincoln won by a huge margin in the Electoral College, receiving 180 electoral votes. However, he got just around 40% of the popular vote, indicating the divided composition of the electorate. Lincoln carried all the free states but did not win a single slave state. His win emphasized the enormous sectional split and laid the scenario for an unparalleled national catastrophe.

The South's Reaction

The response in the South to Lincoln's election was quick and fierce. Southern states had long warned that the election of a Republican president would be an unbearable danger to their way of life and economic interests, which were intrinsically tied to slavery. Lincoln's triumph reinforced their greatest fears: they feared that the federal government would now be governed by Northern forces intent to eradicate slavery.

South Carolina was the first state to act. On December 20, 1860, just a little over a month after the election, South Carolina's legislature voted overwhelmingly to separate from the Union.

The state's Declaration of the Immediate Causes which Induce and Justify the Secession of South Carolina underlined that the election of a president "whose opinions and purposes are hostile to slavery" was a direct assault on their rights and security.

The secession of South Carolina kicked off a chain reaction across the Deep South. By February 1861, Mississippi, Florida, Alabama, Georgia, Louisiana, and Texas had all followed suit.

These states assembled in Montgomery, Alabama, to create the Confederate States of America, choosing Jefferson Davis as their president. They produced a constitution that specifically safeguarded the system of slavery and affirmed the autonomy of states.

The departing president, James Buchanan, proclaimed secession unconstitutional but argued that the federal government lacked the right to push states back into the Union. This approach left the problem unsolved and further strengthened secessionists.

Lincoln, knowing of the combustible situation, kept relatively mute on the question of secession in the months preceding his inauguration. His major objective was to preserve the Union without sparking more conflicts.

In his inauguration speech on March 4, 1861, Lincoln took a conciliatory tone, stressing that he had no desire to interfere with slavery where it remained but also asserting that the Union was everlasting and secession was legally worthless. He appealed to the "better angels of our nature" and highlighted that civil war might be averted via communication and compromise.

However, Lincoln's cry for unity fell on deaf ears in the South. The Confederate States, perceiving his election and subsequent acts as aggressive movements against their sovereignty and way of life, prepared for battle. The situation reached a boiling point on April 12, 1861, when Confederate soldiers fired on Fort Sumter in Charleston Harbor, marking the commencement of the Civil War.

The election of 1860, then, was not merely a political struggle; it was a key event in American history that showed the deep-rooted differences inside the country. Lincoln's elevation to the president and the South's response to it were the last stages on the path to a conflict that would decide the destiny of the United States and the fate of slavery.

Chapter 11: The Final Days of the Union

As the year 1860 concluded, the United States found itself on the edge of a catastrophic shift. The election of Abraham Lincoln in November had functioned as the spark for an already explosive situation, widening a deep breach between the Northern and Southern states.

Lincoln's election, viewed by many in the South as a direct danger to the institution of slavery, pushed South Carolina to take dramatic action. On December 20, 1860, South Carolina seceded from the Union, creating a precedent for other Southern states to follow and marked the beginning of the end for the United States as it had existed since the Revolutionary War.

The mood in December 1860 was one of worry and approaching calamity. South Carolina's choice to secede was not taken lightly, but rather as the result of years of stress and despair.

The state had long been a center of pro-slavery opinion, and its economy was highly based on slave labor. The election of a Republican president who was perceived as opposed to the interests of slaveholders was seen as an existential danger.

In a special convention convened in Charleston, delegates voted unanimously for secession, saying that the Constitution had been violated by the North's position on slavery and that secession was their only choice to protect their rights and way of life.

South Carolina's secession was an important and symbolic act. It was the first state to secede, paving the groundwork for the foundation of the Confederacy. The state's leaders thought they were acting in defense of their rights and freedoms, using the ideals of the Declaration of Independence to defend their actions.

This act of resistance emphasized the vast ideological difference that had formed between the North and South on the subject of slavery and states' rights.

The Immediate Aftermath of Secession

The secession of South Carolina sent shockwaves across the nation. In the immediate aftermath, there was a rush of action and vigorous discussion among other Southern states. The issue was no longer whether they would follow South Carolina's example, but when and how they would do so. The secession movement gathered steam swiftly, fueled by a combination of fear, wrath, and a feeling of unity among the Southern states.

Within weeks, numerous more states had summoned conventions to contemplate secession. Mississippi, Florida, Alabama, Georgia, Louisiana, and Texas all followed South Carolina's example, seceding from the Union by early February 1861.

Each state published its proclamation of independence, frequently claiming the defense of slavery as a main cause. The fast series of sessions showed the intensity of the problem and the feeling of urgency felt by the Southern governments.

In the North, the reaction was one of astonishment and dismay. Many Northerners had not expected that the Southern states would go through with secession. The news of South Carolina's withdrawal from the Union and the succeeding secessions were welcomed with a combination of shock and rage.

President James Buchanan, whose tenure was nearing a conclusion, felt himself essentially helpless to stem the wave of disunion. His government adopted a quiet attitude, assuming that the secession situation was a transient blip that would resolve itself with time. This inactivity only served to encourage the separatist cause.

Amid the political turmoil, there was also a feeling of approaching violence. Federal facilities in the seceding states, including forts and arsenals, were flashpoints. In South Carolina, the situation at Fort Sumter in Charleston Harbor exemplified the rising tension. Major Robert Anderson, the Union commander of Fort Sumter, refused to surrender the fort to the South Carolina militia. This confrontation became a symbol of the greater battle between the Union and the emerging Confederacy.

The Nation on the Brink of War

As additional Southern states joined the secession movement, the Union faced an unprecedented constitutional crisis. By February 1861, officials from the seceding states convened in Montgomery, Alabama, to organize a new government, the Confederate States of America. Jefferson Davis, a former U.S. Senator from Mississippi, was chosen as the

Confederacy's first president. The foundation of the Confederacy cemented the division between North and South, establishing two different governmental entities with opposing ideas on slavery and states' rights.

The country was now on the edge of war. The Lincoln administration, ready to enter office in March 1861, had the mammoth problem of maintaining the Union. Lincoln's viewpoint was clear: he believed secession unconstitutional and was committed to defending the integrity of the United States.

In his inaugural speech, Lincoln attempted to appeal to the seceded states by assuring them that he had no plan to meddle with slavery where it already existed. However, he also made it plain that the Union was permanent and that actions of secession were insurrectionary.

Lincoln's plea for peace and healing was welcomed with a mixed reaction. While some in the North backed his tough attitude, others called for a more conciliatory approach to avert conflict.

In the South, Lincoln's election and his inaugural speech did nothing to relieve worries. Many Southerners considered Lincoln as an opponent of their way of life and thought that war was unavoidable to safeguard their rights and sovereignty.

The situation at Fort Sumter continued to worsen. In April 1861, after months of tension, Confederate soldiers requested the surrender of the fort. When Major Anderson refused, Confederate artillery opened fire on April 12, marking the commencement of the Civil War. The shelling of Fort Sumter energized the North, leading to a wave of patriotism and a call to arms. Lincoln replied by asking for 75,000 volunteers to quash the insurrection, greatly intensifying the fight.

The assault on Fort Sumter had a uniting impact on the North, but it also reinforced the determination of the South. Virginia, Arkansas, North Carolina, and Tennessee, which had been on the borderline regarding secession, joined the Confederacy in the aftermath of Fort Sumter. The boundaries were now clearly established, and the country was thrown into a full-scale civil war.

The closing days of the Union were characterized by a fast and irreversible plunge into war. The events of December 1860 to April 1861 exposed the fundamental differences within the nation and the inability of political settlement. The secession issue and the founding of the Confederacy underlined the vast contrasts in economic interests, social institutions, and political beliefs between the North and South. The nation's leaders, unable to reconcile these differences, found themselves leading their people into the deadliest battle in American history.

The start of the Civil War was a testimony to the fragility of the Union and the volatility of the issues at stake. The contest to determine the nation's destiny, whether as a unified republic or a collection of separate nations, was to be resolved on the battlefield.

The legacy of these closing days of the Union is a sobering reminder of the consequences of separation and the significance of preserving a commitment to democratic values and togetherness.

Conclusion

The decade leading up to the American Civil War was characterized by a succession of significant and controversial events that emphasized the deep-seated differences within the country.

This era, commonly referred to as the "Decade of Disunion," was a time when the United States battled with the moral, political, and economic ramifications of slavery, eventually resulting in the fracturing of the Union. Reflecting on this decade, we may identify some major themes and lessons that remain pertinent to comprehending both the past and the present.

The Mexican War (1846-1848) laid the groundwork for the decade's turbulence. The acquisition of huge new regions prompted significant considerations concerning the extension of slavery. These problems could not be resolved by the existing political system, which had been carefully balancing the interests of free and slave states since the nation's formation.

The Compromise of 1850 was an effort to solve these difficulties, but it only gave a limited relief. It featured the contentious Fugitive Slave Act, which aroused Northern resistance and prepared the ground for more war.

The Kansas-Nebraska Act of 1854, which essentially invalidated the Missouri Compromise, permitted new territories to resolve the question of slavery via popular sovereignty. This led to violent conflicts in

"Bleeding Kansas," a phrase that embodies the savage and fatal fights between pro-slavery and anti-slavery settlers. These episodes were more than isolated instances; they were harbingers of the broader struggle to come, suggesting that compromise was becoming more unsustainable.

The Dred Scott decision of 1857 further split the country. The Supreme Court's judgment that African Americans had no rights as citizens and that Congress had no jurisdiction to ban slavery in the territories shocked the North and encouraged the South.

This judgment not only increased the moral and legal rifts between the two areas but also damaged the political solutions that had previously kept the Union together.

John Brown's attack on Harpers Ferry in 1859 was another spark. Brown's effort to inspire a slave uprising was considered an act of terrorism in the South and martyrdom in the North.

It emphasized the rising militancy of the abolitionist movement and the mounting desperation of those devoted to preserving slavery. Brown's expedition heightened Southern worries of a widespread slave uprising and persuaded many that secession was the only realistic answer to safeguard their way of life.

The election of Abraham Lincoln in 1860 was the last straw for many Southern states. Lincoln's win, without a single Southern electoral vote, emphasized the sectional divide. His program, which opposed the spread of slavery into the new territories, was considered an existential danger to the Southern economy and social order. South Carolina's secession in December 1860, followed by other Southern states, signified the beginning of the end of the Union as it had been known.

The impact of the decade up to the Civil War is diverse, affecting American society, politics, and culture to this day. The most immediate and significant impact, of course, was the Civil War itself.

The battle led to the deaths of nearly 620,000 men, a staggering toll that illustrates the severity and breadth of the struggle. It also led to the abolition of slavery, one of the most momentous societal revolutions in American history.

The events of this decade also laid the foundation for the Reconstruction era, a violent and revolutionary period that tried to reconstruct the South and incorporate formerly enslaved people into American society.

The 13th, 14th, and 15th Amendments to the Constitution, which ended slavery, conferred citizenship, and guaranteed voting rights for African Americans, were direct repercussions of the Civil War and the previous decade of disunion.

Politically, the decade changed the American landscape. The demise of the Whig Party and the development of the Republican Party, which was based on anti-slavery ideals, showed the shifting dynamics and realignments within American politics. This era also witnessed the solidification of sectoral identities, with the North and South creating different political, economic, and social cultures that would continue to emerge in the post-war period.

Culturally, the decade affected literature, art, and public conversation. The abolitionist movement generated strong writings and speeches that continue to reverberate today. Figures like Frederick Douglass, Harriet Beecher Stowe, and William Lloyd Garrison utilized their voices to question the current quo and push for human rights, leaving a lasting influence on American culture and philosophy.

The decade of disunion also emphasized the fragility of democracy. The collapse of political consensus and the resort to violence emphasized the problems of preserving a democratic society in the face of deep-seated differences. This moment serves as a clear reminder of the perils of polarization and the significance of discussion and compromise in preserving a viable democracy.

The events of the decade preceding the Civil War provide some key lessons for current democratic countries. First and foremost, they underline the significance of tackling underlying social and economic inequities.

The inability to overcome the question of slavery, an institution fundamentally at variance with democratic norms, eventually contributed to the nation's disintegration. Modern democracies must confront their systematic disparities and strive towards inclusive solutions that maintain the values of justice and equality.

Another crucial lesson is the significance of political compromise and discussion. The collapse of compromise in the 1850s, symbolized by the Kansas-Nebraska Act and the Dred Scott decision, exposed the perils of rigidity and radicalism.

In today's heated political atmosphere, cultivating a culture of conversation and identifying common ground is crucial to prevent divides from becoming insurmountable.

The decade also illustrates the significance of leadership in times of crisis. Figures like Abraham Lincoln, who steered the country through its worst hour, show the traits of vision, perseverance, and moral clarity that are vital in leaders. Modern democracies demand leaders who can rise above party differences and manage their country through complicated and hard situations.

The necessity of civic involvement and public participation is another lesson from this time. The abolitionist movement, led by passionate and determined people, had a crucial impact in molding public opinion and legislation. Modern democracies thrive upon an engaged and educated public that pushes for justice and keeps leaders responsible.

Finally, the decade of disunion tells us that democracy is not self-sustaining; it takes ongoing attention and work. The circumstances up to the Civil War were a consequence of complacency and a failure to confront basic concerns. Protecting and sustaining democracy needs continual dedication to its ideals, active engagement in its procedures, and a readiness to face and address its issues.

Reflecting on the decade of disunion, we witness a time defined by tremendous strife and significant upheaval. The events of this century, spurred by the unsolved problem of slavery, eventually led to the Civil War and altered the country. The legacy of this decade is reflected in the abolition of slavery, the political realignments, and the cultural upheavals that followed.

For contemporary democracies, the lessons from this time are clear: address fundamental disparities, create conversation and compromise, seek strong and visionary leadership, stimulate civic involvement, and be diligent in defending democratic norms. By learning from the past, we may try to construct a more fair and resilient future.

Made in United States
North Haven, CT
30 November 2024